I BELIEVE

A Collection of Inspiring Declarations
and Uncommon Observations

By RICHARD M. GRANDQUIST

© 2023 by Richard M. Grandquist

Published by Purpose Books, Little Rock, AR

All rights reserved. No part of this publication may be reproduced, stored in a retrieval system, or transmitted in any form or by any means without the prior written permission of the publisher. The only exception is brief quotations in printed reviews.

For information, contact:
Purpose Books
P.O. Box 15561
Little Rock, AR 72231

Edited by: Sweetpea Copeland | Donnie Copeland
Cover design: Robyn Hoffman

To order more books, email:
mgrandquist@gmail.com

Printed in the United States of America

Please consider requesting that a copy of this book be purchased by your local library system.

Library of Congress Control Number: 2023907716

ISBN: 978-1-7331248-5-0

Dedication

I dedicate this book to Thelma Grandquist Venturella, the woman who raised me, my dear mother, the essence of love and generosity.

1. I Believe:
We should go *to* the Lord before we go *for* the Lord.

2. I Believe:
We are called to be holy as our heavenly Father is holy. We should live in such a way that the world sees Him through us.

3. I Believe:
We need to prophesy our praise.

It's not just praising God for what He has done. (past tense) But it's praising God for what He will do. (future tense)

4. I Believe:
We, as holy people, forgive relentlessly—continuously, habitually—because our holy God never fails to forgive us.

5. I Believe:
Holiness is the identity from which we live and the calling we get to live out.

1 Peter 2:9-10 defines who you are: holy, chosen, called, forgiven. Step into the power and the calling you have been given!

6. I Believe:
The peace of God will help you manage pain. And the promises of God will help you overcome it.

7. I Believe:
The cross is not only a bridge that gets us to God, but it's a sledgehammer that breaks down the walls that separate us.

8. I Believe:
A faith that is not dependent on circumstances enables us to "walk by faith, not by sight."

9. I Believe:
People who pray the most often worry the least.

10. I Believe:
You cannot control what happens to you, but you can control how you frame it.

11. I Believe:
We turn into a judge when we know someone else's flaw, but we become a lawyer when they know ours.

12. I Believe:
Discipleship is not the extent of your knowledge but the depth of your love.

13. I Believe:
We shouldn't try to fit God into our plans. We should make our plans around the priority of worship.

14. I Believe:
In the eyes of God, little things are big things. If we do the little things like big things, then God will do big things like they are little things.

15. I Believe:
We should live our lives with the fundamental conviction that God is able. React like a Christian.

16. I Believe:
It's much easier to act like a Christian than it is to react like one. Why? Because most Christians are great actors. They can play the part, but our reactions reveal who we really are.

17. I Believe:
You shouldn't take yourself so seriously and take God very seriously.

18. I Believe:
It's never too late to be who you might have been.

19. I Believe:
Obedience earns compound interest over time. It's called faithfulness. Eventually, the blessings of God will overtake you.

20. I Believe:
The key to prospering is falling out of love with money and falling in love with people who need it.

21. I Believe:
Forgiveness is the way to unplug from the past.

22. I Believe:
When you have a problem in your life that seems impossible to solve, you need to back away from it so you can get perspective. How do you do that? Worship.

23. I Believe:
Happiness comes from what happens to you. Blessing is what happens to you through knowing God.

24. I Believe:
Difficult roads usually lead to beautiful destinations.

25. I Believe:
If you're content to be simply yourself, you will become more than yourself. (Luke 18:14)

26. I Believe:
When you're criticized, don't let it go to your heart. When you're praised, don't let it go to your head.

27. I Believe:
Life sometimes treats us like an unbuckled test dummy in a simulated collision.

28. I Believe:
There is something much better than self-help; it is God's help.

29. I Believe:
"Great faith is a product of great fights. Great testimonies are the outcome of great tests. Great triumphs can only come out of great trials." -- Smith Wigglesworth

"Don't fret or worry. Instead of worrying, pray. Let petitions and praises shape your worries into prayers, letting God know your concerns. Before you know it, a sense of God's wholeness, everything coming together for good, will come and settle you down. It's wonderful what happens when Christ displaces worry at the center of your life." (Philippians 4:6-7 MSG)

30. I Believe:
Faith is the currency of heaven, and prayer is how we exchange sorrow for joy, ashes for beauty, and spiritual deadness for supernatural power.

31. I Believe:
Freedom is hard won and easily lost.

32. I Believe
Every single day, goodness and mercy are following you. Get busy! Get back to what God has called you to do. God's mercy is new every morning.

"Surely goodness and mercy shall follow me all the days of my life." (Psalms 23:6)

33. I Believe:
Passion must marry persistence for us to be consistent. Stay the course. Faithfully keep your time with God. Don't trade that precious communion for anything. Keep on praying, fasting, and sacrificing.

34. I Believe
Without the Holy Spirit people are always inwardly focused, needy, feel entitled, easily offended, overly suspicious, extremely jealous, living for the applause of man, ready to give up upon hearing the slightest criticism and always blaming others.

With the Holy Spirit, people heal the sick, cast out devils, save the lost, impact the world, and disregard what people say about them.

35. I Believe
It's important to know what you believe. But it's more important to know in whom you have believed.

36. I Believe
God gives you His Holy Spirit to sanctify you, and you are called to share in His holiness.

The word "saints" means "holy ones." In the New Testament; it is applied to all Christians. You are "called to be holy." (1 Corinthians 1:2)

37. I Believe:
Obedience earns compound interest. Over time, it's called faithfulness. Eventually, the blessings of God will overtake you.

38. I Believe:
Jesus said, "If? There are no 'ifs' among believers. Anything can happen." (Mark 9:23 MSG)

39. I Believe:
The proof of the Christian is in the living.

40. I Believe:
God says, "You can, in spite of what has been done!" The enemy says, "You can't, because of what you have done!" God will never define you by your past issues, but the enemy will try to confine you by them.

41. I Believe:
God looks at your future, while the enemy tries to keep you in your past.

42. I Believe:
The next time someone hurts you or someone you love, remember the beauty and power of God's grace. Sit in that grace for a while, until it flows from you.

"Summon your power, O God; show us your strength, O God, as you have done before." (Psalm 68:28)

43. I Believe:
"Success consists of going from failure to failure without loss of enthusiasm." -- Winston Churchill

44. I Believe:
Righteousness guards the person of integrity. Integrity does not mean being perfect. It means being honest, real, and authentic. It is the opposite of hypocrisy.

45. I Believe:
Because of God's approval, we aren't insecure or intimidated.

46. I Believe:
When you are generous, you are "enriched." When you "refresh" others, you are "refreshed." (Proverbs 11:25)

"Therefore, I will boast all the more gladly about my weaknesses, so that Christ's power may rest on me. For when I am weak, then I am strong." (2 Cor. 12:9–10)

Don't be self-confident; be God-confident.

When fear knocks on the door of your life, let faith answer!

"For in this unbelieving world you will experience trouble and sorrows, but you must be courageous, for I have conquered the world!" (John 16:33 TPT)

47. I Believe:
The battle we face every day is to trust God's heart and believe Him for the impossible.

48. I Believe
We remember what we should forget, and forget what we should remember.

49. I Believe:
When we praise God, He will show up. When He shows up, it will change our thinking. If we change our thoughts, we change our lives.

50. I Believe:
Our lives follow the direction of our thoughts. The better we grasp that truth, the better equipped we'll be to change the trajectory of our lives.

51. I Believe:
You can run away from what you are afraid of, but you'll be running the rest of your life. It's time to face your fears, take a running leap of faith, and conquer your fears.

52. I Believe:
God orchestrates bad situations to bring good results.

The Bible tells us what Jesus endured to save us: "But He was pierced for our rebellion, crushed for our sins. He was beaten so we could be whole. He was whipped so we could be healed. ... He was oppressed and treated harshly, yet He never said a word. He was led like a lamb to the slaughter. And as a sheep is silent before the shearers, He did not open His mouth." (Isaiah 53:4-7 NLT)

53. I Believe:
You should burn sinful bridges. Blaze new trails.

54. I Believe:
We should quit holding out, quit holding back, quit running away. Do something for God.

55. I Believe:
Dysfunctional relationships can suck you dry. True forgiveness is the only way to survive a vampire attack.

56. I Believe:
Don't let what's wrong with you keep you from worshiping what's right with God.

"The Lord is close to the broken-hearted and saves those who are crushed in spirit." (Psalm 34:18)

When you are going through a difficult time, you may not necessarily feel God is close, but He is. "God is there every time." (Psalm 34:19 MSG)

57. I Believe:
When you leave this earth, you can take nothing you have received, but only what you have been given.

The Spirit of God has made me, and the breath of the Almighty gives me life. (Job 33:4 ESV)

"My definition of success: Do the best you can with what you have where you are." -- Richard M Grandquist II

58. I Believe:
Life is not a competition that you have to win. It is not supposed to be a rat race. Life is a huge privilege and an opportunity.

God has trusted you with gifts and abilities which he wants you to use. Use them or lose them. He is faithful to us and He expects us to be faithful to him.

59. I Believe:

In all your relationships – especially when you encounter great difficulties – you should imitate God. Be "gracious and compassionate, slow to anger and rich in love."

Oh, "the wonder of [God's] great love." (Psalm 17:7)

60. I Believe:

It is the power of God that makes what seems impossible possible. Nothing is impossible with God.

61. I Believe:

You are not the mistakes you've made. You are not the labels put on you by other people. You are who God says you are. Anything less is false humility.

Charles Spurgeon, the great preacher who suffered from depression and anxiety, said, "I have learned to kiss the wave that throws me against the Rock of Ages." That is easier said than done, no doubt. But that is how spiritual growth happens.

62. I Believe:

If you fear God, you need not fear anything else or anyone else.

63. I Believe:
Worship begins in holy expectancy and worship ends in holy obedience.

64. I Believe:
Whatever challenges you may face in the year ahead, nothing is too hard for the Lord.

The Merchant of Venice (Act IV Scene 1):
"The quality of mercy is not strain'd,
It droppeth as the gentle rain from heaven
Upon the place beneath: it is twice blest;
It blesseth him that gives and him that takes."

65. I Believe:
A pure heart starts with your thoughts because your thoughts become your words, your actions, and your character.

In *A Christmas Carol* by Charles Dickens, the central character, Ebenezer Scrooge, was a miserable, mean, miserly old businessman who is shown his past, present and future. He eventually repents and starts to give generously. Dickens captures the transformation in his character. "He went to church and walked about the streets… and found that everything could yield him pleasure. He had never dreamed that any walk – that anything – could give him so much happiness."

Repentance and church will do that for you.

66. I Believe:
During the Christmas season, we need to celebrate relationships and show love to people to whom we're deeply connected.

"Christmas is a season of not only rejoicing, but of reflection." — Winston Churchill

"And God will wipe away every tear from their eyes." (Revelation 7:17)

Thankfully, God makes it all better in the end.

67. I Believe:
We need each other more than ever right now.

The Bible is full of "one-another" statements that we can only accomplish with...one another.

Love one another (John 13:34) • Serve one another (Galatians 5:13) • Forgive one another (Ephesians 4:32) • Honor one another (Romans 12:10) • Pray for one another (James 5:16)

68. I Believe:
God loves you unconditionally, wholeheartedly, and continually.

"God is love." (1 John 4:8,16)

The word "love" is used widely in our society. Nowhere in the Bible does it say, "love is God."

In other words, it is God who defines what love is rather than the other way around. God is love.

69. I Believe:
Love God like your soul depends on it. Love people like your life depends on it.

"When good people run things, everyone is glad, but when the ruler is bad, everyone groans." (Proverbs29:2, MSG)

70. I Believe:
Regret looks back. Fear looks around. Worry looks in. Faith looks up.

Don't be put off by fear, which leads to inertia and lack of activity. Jesus sets us free to advance without fear of the opposition. (Proverbs 26:13,14)

71. I Believe:
"Your life as a Christian should make non-believers question their disbelief in God." – Dietrich Bonhoeffer

72. I Believe:
"Love makes you real." (The Velveteen Rabbit)

73. I Believe:
Your life has a purpose. Your story is important. Your dreams count. Your voice matters. You were born to make an impact.

"Never give in. Never give in. Never, never, never, never – in nothing, great or small, large or petty – never give in, except to convictions of honor and good sense. Never yield to force. Never yield to the apparently overwhelming might of the enemy." -- Sir Winston Churchill

74. I Believe:
During life's difficulties and extraordinary challenges, JESUS is the empowering presence who brings us peace.

75. I Believe:
If your life is to be fruitful, you must stay faithful to God in the difficult times.

76. I Believe:
"Holiness is a furnace that transforms the men and women who enter it." -- Eugene Peterson

77. I Believe:
If you know how to worry, you know how to meditate! All you need to do is change what you think about, and you will be practicing Christian meditation.

What Paul writes applies to us all: "Keep your eyes open. Hold tight to your convictions, give it all you've got, be resolute and love without stopping." (1 Corinthians 16:13–14, MSG).

"… if my people, who are called by my name, will humble themselves and pray and seek my face and turn from their wicked ways, then will I hear from heaven and will forgive their sin and will heal their land." (2 Chronicles 7:14)

These are the conditions necessary for revival. We see in this verse that we need to do four things:
- Humble ourselves
- Pray
- Seek God's face
- Turn from our wicked ways.

Then God promises that he will do three things:
- Hear from Heaven
- Forgive our sin
- Heal the land.

78. I Believe:
- You must learn who you are to learn who you're not.
- You are not what others think about you.
- You are not your past.
- You are not what you did.
- You are who God says you are.

The Psalmist writes, "You grant… relief from days of trouble… When I said, 'My foot is slipping,' your love, O Lord, supported me. When anxiety was great within me, your consolation brought joy to my soul." (Psalms 94:12-23)

79. I Believe:
You are far more valuable to God than the wrongs that you have committed.

80. I Believe:
If you want to keep the right perspective, keep your eyes fixed on Jesus and keep worshipping and serving your creator.

Here's a prayer I think we should all be praying:
Lord, as we look around at the state of our cities, our nation and our world, we need Your deliverance. You alone are God over all the kingdoms of the earth. You made heaven and earth. Give ear, O Lord, and hear; open your eyes, O Lord, and see. Pour out your Holy Spirit again. May we see people seeking Your name again. May we see miracles of healing. May we see the evangelization of our nation, the revitalization of the church and the transformation of society, so that all kingdoms on earth may know that You alone, O Lord, are God.

81. I Believe:
Your face often reflects your heart. A happy heart makes the face cheerful.
It's been said that the life we live eventually shows on our face and, therefore, everybody over 40 is responsible for their face!

Psalms 66:1-12
God had brought his people through very difficult times.

"He trained us first, passed us like silver through refining fires...pushed us to our very limit, road-tested us inside and out, took us to hell and back; Finally, he brought us to this well-watered place." (vv.10–12, MSG)

82. I Believe:

However down you might feel about a circumstance, however far from God you may feel, however difficult you may find it to pray, whatever doubts you have, the Spirit of the Lord is upon you. You are being transformed into his likeness and God is with you.

83. I Believe:

Hope is the confident expectation of God's ultimate blessing in this life and the life to come, based upon the goodness and promises of God.

84. I Believe:

When we judge, accuse, and condemn others, we project on to them what we refuse to see in ourselves.

It's been said that our mistakes define us, but I believe what we do to right them is what defines us.

85. I Believe:

We tend to look for the perfect spouse, perfect parents, perfect children, perfect friends, perfect leaders, and the perfect church. But these don't exist. All of us are flawed human beings. Recognizing this helps us to be more realistic, less disappointed, and more forgiving in our relationships.

86. I Believe:
Jesus transforms drudgery and dreariness into fullness of joy.

"Do not be afraid; do not be discouraged…" (Joshua 8:1)

87. I Believe:
We should live from hand to mouth. It's my mouth asking for God's help, and it's His hand that gives it to me.

"The Lord bless you and keep you; the Lord make his face shine on you and be gracious to you; the Lord turn his face towards you and give you peace." (Numbers 6:24-26 NIV)

"I've put my life in your hands. You won't drop me, you'll never let me down." (Psalm 31:5, MSG)

I love the fact that God won't drop us.

"The Lord gives strength to his people' and 'blesses his people with peace." (Psalm 29:11)

Lord, thank you for sharing with us your authority, power, and strength. Please strengthen me for the battles of today and give me peace during the storms of life.

Don't waste your time hanging around people who try to belittle your dreams. Associate with people who inspire and challenge you, lift you higher and make you better. Walk with the visionaries, the believers, the doers and the courageous. Great people make you feel that you too can become great.

Stir one another up to pray, serve and give.

88. I Believe:
Faith is climbing out on a limb, cutting it off and watching the tree fall.

"When you are up in life, your friends get to know who you are. When you are down in life, you get to know who your friends are!" – Nancy Grandquist

89. I Believe:
First comes God's call and vision; then follows all the challenges and difficulties before you see the promise fulfilled.

God's way is not always easy. It is extraordinarily challenging, but at the end of the day, wonderfully fulfilling.

90. I Believe:
Every experience is preparation for some future opportunity.

91. I Believe:
Jesus doesn't just set us free from who we were. He sets us free to become who we were meant to be.

92. I Believe:
Salvation is not the end goal. Salvation is a new beginning.

God is fair
If you are suffering here on earth, you may think God is not fair, but God has all eternity to make it up to you!

See the suffering of this life in the realm of eternity by standing at the edge of the temporal and looking into the light of eternity. – Nancy Grandquist

"You intended to harm me, but God intended it for good to accomplish what is now being done, the saving of many lives." (Genesis 50:20)

When we are mistreated in any way, we must realize our suffering has profound and vast implications for the greater kingdom of God. There are unseen reasons for continued suffering. Who knows what God will do with your life if you take mistreatment with grace and humility.

"He who has felt the deepest grief is best able to experience supreme happiness." -- Alexandre Dumas.

93. I Believe:
You owe it to yourself to be yourself, but more importantly, you owe it to your Creator, the One who designed you.

94. I Believe:

There is nothing God cannot do in you and through you. If you simply yield your life to Him.

Noah was 600 years old when he began his life's work. It proves it's never too late for God to use you, no matter how old you are.

95. I Believe:

True spirituality is the place where desperation meets Jesus. The path of least resistance never gets us where we want to go. Shortcuts always end up being cul-de-sacs.

96. I Believe:

We need to go after a dream that is destined to fail without divine intervention.

Everything will be all right in the end. If it's not all right, then it is not the end. These words convey a profound theological truth.

Run the race to the end.

97. I Believe:

We can become the kind of container God can use to present any and every kind of gift to His guests for their blessing. (2 Timothy 2:20–21, MSG)

98. I Believe:
We are not cowards if we feel afraid. In fact, there can be no courage unless you are scared. Courage is doing what you are afraid to do, and not allowing fear to rule your decisions.

"Everyone goes down fool's hill but only fools set up camp." -- I.H. Terry

"If you think you're too small to make a difference, you haven't spent the night with a mosquito." – African proverb

"… one thing I do: Forgetting what is behind and straining towards what is ahead…" (Philippians 3:13b)

99. I Believe:
The battle is won or lost in our minds. It is essential that we "take captive every thought to make it obedient to Christ."

100. I Believe:
We worship, not because we necessarily feel like it, nor because things are going well. In fact, sometimes we worship despite difficult circumstances and hard times.

101. I Believe:
Holiness is linked to wholeness. When God calls you to be holy, He is saying, "be wholly mine."

102. I Believe:
To live without hope is to cease to live.

103. I Believe:
God wants you to offer all of yourself – your time, ambitions, possessions, ears, mouth – as well as your mind, emotions, and attitudes.

104. I Believe:
Salvation is based on:
- Faith – not your good works
- Mercy – not what you deserve
- Belief – not where you were born

God calls us to "sow for yourselves righteousness" and "reap the fruit of unfailing love… for it is time to seek the Lord." (Hosea 10:12)

105. I Believe:
When we live for ourselves, it is a form of slavery that only living for Jesus can free you from.

My definition of grace is "undeserved love." Show love to people who least expect it.

Grace is loving people for who they are and where they are. It's loving people before they change, not just after they change. And that grace is the difference between holy and holier-than-thou.

106. I Believe:
At the end of the day, faith is trusting God more than you trust your assumptions.

Do not be discouraged. Keep on praying with faith and boldness, love, and sensitivity.

107. I Believe:
Things work out when you trust in God. (Proverbs 16:20)

Trust that God is in control.

Faith means trusting God. C.S. Lewis wrote that "faith is the art of holding on to things your reason has once accepted, in spite of your changing moods."

It is difficult to trust God when everything seems to be going wrong, but trust God anyway.

"Commit to the Lord whatever you do, and your plans will succeed." (Proverbs 16:1,3)

108. I Believe:
God turns the ordinary into the extraordinary.

The three conversions: to be converted to Christ, converted to His church, and converted to His cause.

109. I Believe:
Whatever you are facing – a difficult boss, a complicated marriage, raising a problematic child – God gives you strength to stick with it.

110. I Believe:
We lose perspective when we lose sight of the promises of God.

You can praise God before, during and after battles you face. "I'll never run out of praise." (Psalm 71:8)

111. I Believe:
Everything we have belongs to God. He wants to be involved in all our lives.

Through the Holy Spirit living within us, we are empowered to become like Jesus in all our thoughts, attitudes, words, and actions. We are Jesus to the world.

112. I Believe:
A person with integrity has the often-rare ability to pull everything together, to make it all happen no matter how challenging the circumstances.

113. I Believe:
"Forgiveness is like fresh air to the soul. Breathe in deeply and live free." – Nancy Grandquist

114. I Believe:
God always puts us around someone who is like sandpaper to smooth off our rough edges.

115. I Believe:
Disunity destroys. Love unites.

116. I Believe:
- You reap what you sow.
- You reap later than you sow.
- You reap more than you sow.
- We should be thoughtful of what we sow.

117. I Believe:
If we love, like Jesus, we will neither condone sin nor condemn people, but lovingly challenge people (starting with ourselves) to leave sin behind.

"Do not worry about what other people think. What God thinks is what matters. Encounter Jesus again today and enjoy the full, abundant, spacious, open-hearted, high-definition life which Jesus offers." – Nancy Grandquist

118. I Believe:
We should overlook insults rather than showing our annoyance.

"Fools have short fuses and explode all too quickly; the prudent quietly shrug off insults." (Proverbs 12:10 MSG)

119. I Believe:
We are created to live in a relationship with God. Without that, life will never really make sense. Misery will be our companion.

120. I Believe:
God turns your weakness into strength. God gives "endless energy, boundless strength!" (Ephesians 1:19)

121. I Believe:
Sometimes you may face difficulties not because you are doing something wrong but because you are doing something right.

122. I Believe:
"A generous person will prosper; whoever refreshes others will be refreshed." (Proverbs 11:25)

123. I Believe:
Who you become is determined by how you pray. Ultimately, the transcript of your prayers becomes the script of your life.

124. I Believe:
Many conflicts could be avoided if people would talk to each other, rather than just talk about each other.

125. I Believe:
Righteousness is ultimately about right relationships – a right relationship with God and right relationships with others.

126. I Believe:
"There are only two ways to live your life. One is as though nothing is a miracle. The other is as though everything is a miracle." – Albert Einstein

Do you realize that God is with you? And if God is with you, then you can face every challenge that lies ahead.

127. I Believe:
Your words are powerful. With kind and encouraging words, you can change a person's day, or even his entire life.

128. I Believe:
Worship saves us from being self-centered and makes us God-centered.

129. I Believe:
Truth becomes hard if it is not softened by love. Love becomes soft if it is not strengthened by truth.

130. I Believe:
Life is too short to worry about stupid things. Pray. Trust God. Enjoy life. Don't let the little things get you down.

131. I Believe:
Jesus sees your heart rather than your past.

132. I Believe:
Happiness is dependent on what happens – our circumstances. Joy is far deeper and is not so dependent on our outward circumstances.

133. I Believe:
When we pray, God hears more than we say, answers more than we ask, gives more than we imagine – in His own time and in His own way.

134. I Believe:
The amazing truth is that our Heavenly Father is merciful and gives us love and protection, even when we don't deserve it.

135. I Believe:
Forgiveness sometimes takes great courage, but it restores relationships and brings great joy.

It is said that the first to apologize is the bravest, the first to forgive is the strongest, and the first to forget is the happiest.

136. I Believe:
Holiness and wholeness are closely related. God wants the whole of your life.

137. I Believe:
What cannot be achieved by addition, God does by multiplication.

138. I Believe:
What you give to God, He multiplies.

139. I Believe:
We all have good intentions, but we are all flawed. We can't follow through without the power of God.

140. I Believe:
A failed attempt is not failing. Failing is not trying. If you are trying, you are succeeding.

141. I Believe:
As you draw close to God in intimate friendship, His concerns become your concerns.

142. I Believe:
Strength grows through struggles, courage develops in challenges, and wisdom matures from wounds.

143. I Believe:
If you stay faithful to God, you can experience His presence, His favor, and His blessing.

144. I Believe:
You should plan and think ahead, but don't worry ahead. Trust in your Heavenly Father to provide.

"Lead me, O Lord, in your righteousness. Make straight your way before me." (Psalm 5:8)

145. I Believe:
God's desire for you is that you walk humbly in a relationship with Him. You may stumble from time to time, but one day you will walk with Him "dressed in white." (Revelation 3:4)

146. I Believe:
The Bible is one long invitation to come to Jesus. In Him, you find the meaning and purpose of your life.

Part of that purpose is to invite others to come, so that they too will find refreshment and fulfilment in the water of life that Jesus pours out on all who come to him.
The Holy Spirit and the church invite people to come and to receive the amazing gifts God has for them.

Revelation 22:7,12,20
No wonder that "the Spirit and the bride [the church] say, 'Come!' And let those who hear say, 'Come!' Let those who are thirsty come; and let all who wish take the free gift of the water of life." (v.17)

147. I Believe:
Jesus sees your heart rather than your past.

You may not have had a good beginning in life, but this does not mean you cannot have a great finish. You do not need to go around burdened by guilt from previous relationships or from incidents in your past.

148. I Believe:
Holiness is about living an integrated life rather than a disintegrated one.

It has been said that everyone has three lives – a public life, a private life, and a secret life. Holiness is where there is no difference between our public, private and secret lives, and no difference between what we profess and what we practice.

149. I Believe:
It is often in times of difficulty that we put down deep roots.

The psalmist uses the evocative expression "deep calls to deep." (Psalm 42:7).

Anything that is not from the depth in us will not reach the depth in others.

150. I Believe:
We must live a life of persistence. A river cuts through rock not because of its power but because of its persistence.

151. I Believe:
We need to Know who God is.

Moses asked God, "Who am I, that I should go?" God replied by telling him who He is.

In the end, the answer to all our questions and problems is not to be found in who we are but in who God is. When you know 'I AM WHO I AM' is with you, you can relax and be at peace. (Exodus 1:1-3)

152. I Believe:

You are God's magnum opus. His greatest masterpiece.

153. I Believe:

We need to wait on God.

During the waiting period, the challenge is to keep on trusting God. Trust God completely today.

154. I Believe:

We should store God's Word in our heart.

Do you long to know God better? Would you like to be wiser, more skillful, and have more knowledge and understanding? Make a lifelong, daily habit of reading God's Word.

The writer of Proverbs urges, "store up my commands within you, turning your ear to wisdom and applying your heart to understanding… For wisdom will enter your heart." (Proverbs 2:1-2 NIV)

155. I Believe:
We need to speak life out of the overflow of God's Word.

Matthew 12:34–35
Jesus says, "… out of the overflow of the heart the mouth speaks. Good people bring good things out of the good stored up in them, and evil people bring evil things out of the evil stored up in them." (vv.34–35)

Speak today out of the overflow of God's Word.

156. I Believe:
Our desire to do what is right in the eyes of God is motivated by the fact that we are the apple of His eye.

So, integrity begins with a fear for God and ends with a love for God.

157. I Believe:
Pride is a by-product of insecurity.

The more insecure you are, the more monuments you'll have to build to yourself, instead of building altars to God.

158. I Believe:

Worship brings joy and pleasure, and it is an appropriate response to such an amazing God.

Psalm 144:1–2

What battles are you fighting in your life? Temptation? Anxiety? Fear? Depression? Financial battles? Health battles? Work or relationship battles?

If you're facing a frightening battle, praise the Lord: "my Rock," "Fortress," "Stronghold," "Deliverer," "my Shield in whom I take refuge' (vv.1–2).

The Lord is powerful. He is also "my loving God." He involves you in His plan; "He trains me to fight fair and well." (v.1, MSG)

You are a partner with God. God, of course, is the major partner but you have a part to play as well.

159. I Believe:

We should be authentic. Holiness does not mean perfection. It means living a life of integrity. It's the opposite of hypocrisy. It means being real, honest, and authentic.

160. I Believe:

We forget what we should remember and remember what we should forget.

Try to remember the good and forget the bad.

161. I Believe:
What you can do for God isn't nearly as important as simply appreciating what God has done for you!

162. I Believe:
In life, you'll offend somebody. Make sure that somebody isn't the Almighty.

163. I Believe:
Integrity begins with the fear of God, but it ends with a love for God.

164. I Believe:
The fear of God is the sign of a fine-tuned conscience.

165. I Believe:
We should keep praying.

Don't lose heart. Don't lose hope. Don't lose faith. Don't lose patience. And keep asking. Keep seeking. Keep knocking.

166. I Believe:
To see yourself as anything other than God's masterpiece is to devalue and distort your true identity. It's in discovering your true identity that your true destiny is revealed.

"We are God's masterpiece. He has created us anew in Christ Jesus, so we can do the good things he planned for us long ago." (Ephesians 2:10, NLT)

167. I Believe:
"You wouldn't care what people thought about you if you knew how seldom they did." -- St. Jean

168. I Believe:
When you lose your way spiritually, the way forward is often backwards.... back to the altar...back to that place in God that filled you with wonder.

169. I Believe:
We should ask ourselves the question, 'What difference has Jesus made?"

The difference Jesus has made in me is massive, eternal, and impossible to comprehend fully.

170. I Believe:
You're in Christ Jesus (Ephesians 1:3). In Christ Jesus, you have received "every spiritual blessing."

171. I Believe:
God loves you, and you love God. And that's what really matters.

It's not complicated. Keep it simple.

172. I Believe:
The heart of Christianity is compassion. The soul of Christianity is wonder. The mind of Christianity is curiosity. The strength of Christianity is energy. – Mark Batterson

173. I Believe:
Love takes pleasure in the flowering of truth. (1 Cor13:1-3)

174. I Believe:
This life is a series of problem-solving exercises. We will never be without problems in this life. In the midst of all the challenges, you can thrive with God on your side.

175. I Believe:
In difficult times, you may sometimes feel that God has left you.

In these times, listen to God's promises over and above your feelings and emotions.

176. I Believe:

God is for you!

177. I Believe:

God loves:
- Keeping promises
- Answering prayers
- Performing miracles
- Fulfilling dreams

178. I Believe:

Three tenses of salvation:
- You HAVE BEEN saved from the PENALTY of sin.
- You WILL BE saved from the PRESENCE of sin.
- You ARE BEING saved from the POWER of sin.

179. I Believe:

Grace is not an excuse to sin. It is a reason *not* to sin.

180. I Believe:

If something matters to you, it matters to God.

181. I Believe:
"The only question on God's final exam is: Do you believe this?" – Mark Batterson

It's the most important question you'll ever answer. That one decision will determine your eternal destiny. Because if you believe, you will receive.

182. I Believe:
If I've had any success, I attribute it to praying and obeying the Lord.

I have always offered myself to follow God's will to its entirety.

"I desire to do your will, O my God; your law is within my heart." (Psalm 40:7)

Let the Word of God transform you. We all need the transforming power of God's word in so many ways. Whether you are seeking wisdom in stressful and complex situations, encouragement when you are downhearted, or guidance on the way forward, you can find help in the pages of the Bible.

183. I Believe:
There are two possible attitudes when facing a giant. One is to say, "It's so big, there's nothing I can do." The other is to say, "It's so big, I can't miss!"

184. I Believe:
When we bow to what's wrong, we put our reputation and God's reputation at risk. But when we stand up for what's right, we establish God's reputation by putting ourselves in a posture where God can show up and show off.

185. I Believe:
Love is more than a feeling or an emotion. It is a decision about how we treat one another.

186. I Believe
Our faith should not be marginalized.

187. I Believe:
Prayerless pulpits will produce prayerless and powerless congregations.

188. I Believe:
Every prayer is a calculated risk. Prayer is how we put the ball into God's court. The only way you can fail is by failing to ask.

189. I Believe:
Those who finish well will always have an unfinished agenda. You will be able to say, "It's not over."

190. I Believe:
Until God opens the door, you should praise Him in the hallway.

191. I Believe:
"There are five main ways in which God guides us (the five CSs):
- Commanding Scripture (the Bible)
- Compelling Spirit (the Holy Spirit)
- Counsel of the Saints (the church)
- Common Sense (reason)
- Circumstantial Signs (providence)."

– Nancy Grandquist

192. I Believe:
God's purpose for you is bigger than your mistakes.

I have made many mistakes in my life, but God has not stopped guiding me.

193. I Believe:
All leadership requires courage to cling tenaciously to a vision, and toughness to endure the blame for every difficulty along the way.

194. I Believe:
People wrapped up in themselves make very small packages.

195. I Believe:
The presence of God will always satisfy our deepest need.

196. I Believe:
"It is a modern tragedy that despair has so many spokesmen, and hope so few." – Oscar Hammerstein II

As The Piano Guys song says, "It's Gonna Be Okay."

197. I Believe:
"Things that matter most should never be at the mercy of things which matter least." – Johann Wolfgang von Goethe

198. I Believe:
The antidote to discontent is thanksgiving.

Cultivate an attitude of gratitude.

199. I Believe:
God's grace is the knot at the end of the rope. It's the only thing that we can grasp that will prevent spiritual freefall.

200. I Believe:
Faith is like a muscle. It grows by stretching.

Stretch today do something for God.

201. I Believe:
Faith is to believe what we do not see. The reward of faith is to see what we believe.

202. I Believe:
The key to a successful Christian life is not to compare, but simply to get on with whatever God calls you to do.

203. I Believe:
Moments of vulnerability make us or break us spiritually. It's precisely in these times that we discover new dimensions of God's grace.

204. I Believe:
If God does not keep a record of your wrongdoings, you should not keep lists of other people's offenses against you. Love "keeps no record of wrongs." (1 Corinthians 13:5)

205. I Believe:
Vision is a 'holy discontent' – a deep dissatisfaction with what is, combined with a clear grasp of what could be. It is a picture – 'a mental sight' – of the future that inspires hope.

Vision without action is merely a dream. Action without vision is a nightmare! But vision combined with action can change the world.

206. I Believe:
Holiness is not boring.

"How little people know who think that holiness is dull. When one meets the real thing... it is irresistible." – C.S. Lewis

207. I Believe:
"Every storm is a school. Every trial is a test. Every experience is an education. Every difficulty is for your development." – Nicky Gumbel

208. I Believe:
"If I were to let my life be taken over by what is urgent, I might very well never get around to what is essential." – Henry Nouwen

209. I Believe:
We should refuse to remember something God has chosen to forget.

210. I Believe:
Faith that has not been tested cannot be trusted.

211. I Believe:
We need to share the wealth.

"Money is like manure. It's not good unless it is spread around." – Francis Bacon

It has been said that a great oak is only a little nut that held its ground. Keep holding on. You'll get there.

212. I Believe:
"The ultimate measure of a person is not where they stand in moments of convenience, but where they stand in moments of challenge, moments of great crisis and controversy." – Dr. Martin Luther King, Jr.

"I live as though Jesus Christ had been crucified yesterday, had risen this morning and was coming again tomorrow."
– Martin Luther

213. I Believe:
Without Him, we cannot. Without us, He will not.

214. I Believe:
We should always remember that hurting people hurt people.

215. I Believe:
"Contentment makes poor men rich; discontent makes rich men poor." -- American Statesman, Benjamin Franklin.

216. I Believe:
"Everyone wants a miracle, but no one wants to be in a situation that necessitates one." – Mark Batterson

"The Bible tells us to love our neighbors, and also to love our enemies; probably because they are generally the same people!" -- G. K. Chesterton

217. I Believe:
"The river of the Spirit of God overcomes all obstacles." -- Oswald Chambers.

Jesus said that the Holy Spirit within you would be like "rivers of living water." (John 7:38)

What do we do when we are at our "wits' end?" (Psalm 107:27). How do we respond to a "black day" in our lives? (Isaiah 37:3, MSG).

Find encouragement in Psalms 107:23-32 and in these answers:
- Cry out to the Lord in prayer. (Galatians 2:1-10)
- Use skill, diplomacy, and courage. (Isaiah 36:1-37:38)
- Bring to the Lord the impossible situation.

218. I Believe:
If I worship in my weakness, His power is made perfect in weakness.

"My grace is sufficient for you, for my power is made perfect in weakness." (2 Corinthians 12:9)

219. I Believe:
God's peace comes to you even in the dark places – during your most difficult struggles and challenges.

220. I Believe:
"When wealth is lost, nothing is lost; when health is lost, something is lost; when character is lost, all is lost."
-- Billy Graham

221. I Believe:
You should do your best and prepare for the worst. Then trust God to bring the victory.

222. I Believe:
Sometimes we hit a wall of pain and distress that overwhelms us. It could be caused by bereavement, sickness, disappointment, or other circumstances beyond our control. What matters most is how we respond to it. It can transform us into people who God can use powerfully.

223. I Believe:
We need to keep all God's salvation stories fresh and present. (Micah 6:5 MSG)

224. I Believe:
In God's love, we find relief, consolation, and joy. God provides "a circle of quiet within the clamor of evil." (Psalm 94:13)

225. I Believe:
A father's heart should be gentle, kind, nurturing, training, persevering, and should never give up on people.

226. I Believe:
If God is with you then you can face every challenge that lies ahead.

227. I Believe:
We can trust God to rescue us, even when it seems difficult to keep trusting in God.

If things go wrong in your relationships, work, finances, health, or some other situation, David's prayer can serve as an encouragement to cry out to God to rescue you and then to put your trust in God. (Psalms 31:1-8)

David prayed, "Turn your ear to me, come quickly to my rescue." (Psalm 31:2)

"I trust in, rely on, and confidently lean on the Lord." (Psalm 31:6, AMP)

In Jesus, you receive the ultimate rescue.

228. I Believe:
God will lift our heaviness and give us His Joy.

"You have turned my mourning into joyful dancing. You have taken away my clothes of mourning and clothed me with joy." (Psalm 30:11, NLT)

229. I Believe:
Righteousness means a right relationship with God. That leads to right relationships with others.

230. I Believe:
"The smile is the beginning of love." -- Mother Teresa

231. I Believe:
We should never let our past limit our future.

232. I Believe:
With Jesus, failure is never final.

233. I Believe:
Being with God is even more important than what you do for God. With God, everything is possible.

234. I Believe:
God uses cracked pots to fulfill His purpose. When held up to God's light, we're all a little cracked.

235. I Believe:
The answer to fear is trusting in God.

"The Lord Almighty is with us." (Psalm 46:7)

"In God I have put my trust and confident reliance; I will not be afraid." (Psalms 56:6,11)

"Darkness cannot drive out darkness; only light can do that. Hate cannot drive out hate; only love can do that."
– Martin Luther King, Jr.

236. I Believe:
If we will honor and trust the Lord, we will never miss out on anything good. (Psalms 34:9,10 CEVUK)

237. I Believe:
If someone has offended you, don't return the offense. Holding a grudge is like letting someone live rent-free in your head.

238. I Believe:
Honesty and integrity are key to a life without regret.

"Ill-gotten gain gets you nowhere; an honest life is immortal." (Proverbs 10:2 MSG)

239. I Believe:
We must "keep our eyes on the prize." And HOLD ON!

240. I Believe:
Courage is not the absence of fear but triumph over it.

241. I Believe:
"Resentment is like drinking poison and hoping it will kill your enemies." – Nelson Mandela

Be like Jesus. Be generous to everyone.

"Our father is kind; you be kind." (Luke 6:36)

242. I Believe:
Life is not easy. We may face battles, opposition and even depression. The right response is to turn to God.

Pray for God's guidance, and His presence, His "joy and delight." (Psalms 43:1-4)

243. I Believe:
God's blessing of protection doesn't depend on us always getting it right. (Psalm 41:4)

244. I Believe:
The key to blessing is generosity.

"The righteous give generously." (Psalm 37:21)

245. I Believe:
"Jesus walking on the earth is more important than man walking on the moon." – Astronaut James Irwin

246. I Believe:
At the end of the day, we all need mercy more than justice.

God is "rich in mercy." (Ephesians 2:4)

A man was having his portrait painted by a successful artist. When the portrait was finished it was unveiled. The man was most unhappy with the result. When asked if he liked it, he replied, "I don't think it does me justice." The artist replied, "Sir, it is not justice you need, but mercy!" The artist was painting Winston Churchill.

Today, we need mercy, not justice.

247. I Believe:
A just God cannot bless unjust transactions.

248. I Believe:
When under attack, we should stand with integrity, uprightness, and faith.

Do the right thing regardless of what people say or think.

249. I Believe:
You are simply called to do the best you can with what you have where you are.

250. I Believe:
Faith doesn't change my circumstances. Faith changes me. And because I'm changed, my circumstances many times change.

251. I Believe:
If you feed your faith, your doubts will starve to death.

"One of the tragedies of our life is that we keep forgetting who we are." – Henri Nouwen

252. I Believe:
Wisdom will keep you steering on the right paths. It will "keep your feet on the tried-and-true paths." It will keep you walking with those who "walk straight."

253. I Believe:
In difficult times:
- Keep praying.
- Keep trusting.
- Keep rejoicing.
- Keep worshipping.

254. I Believe:
The plans of God are only revealed in the presence of God. You don't get your marching orders until you hit your knees.

255. I Believe:
You shouldn't defend yourself against criticism. Life is too short, and the mission is too important. You're called to play offense, not defense.

256. I Believe:
We should walk into every new day with our heads held high, and our eyes fixed on Jesus. – Nancy Grandquist

257. I Believe:
Amazing things happen when we deeply commit our lives to God.

"Consecrate yourself, for tomorrow the Lord will do amazing things among you." (Joshua 3:5)

258. I Believe:
Whatever your past, however broken your life may seem right now, God can use you to do something great with your life.

259. I Believe:
Memory management is important. How you manage your memories will determine:
- How you see life.
- How you see yourself.
- And how you see the future.

260. I Believe:
The key to spiritual growth is being desperate for God. You will find God in uncomfortable places. You will find God at inconvenient times.

261. I Believe:
"When you pray to God regularly, irregular things happen on a regular basis." – Mark Batterson

262. I Believe:
Joy is the remedy for selfishness.

263. I Believe:
Peace is the remedy for conflict.

For better or for worse, I'm just a pastor. Not a confronter. Not a critic. Not a gifted person. Just a pastor trying to be more like Jesus.

264. I Believe:
Worshippers don't focus on what's wrong in their lives. They focus on what's right with God.

265. I Believe:
Worshipping God when everything is going wrong is the purest form of praise.

266. I Believe:
"Although the world is full of suffering, it is also full of overcoming it." – Helen Keller

267. I Believe:
If you want to get out of a spiritual slump, change something up. Pray more. Volunteer. Give more.

268. I Believe:
You shouldn't let anyone label you beside the One who made you.

269. I Believe:
When you cast your care, you lose your despair.

270. I Believe:
"All is well, however hard the wind blows." – C.H. Spurgeon

271. I Believe:
If you're on God's side, God will fight for you as you fight for Him.

272. I Believe:
Your prayers that you prayed last year are still alive. Your prayers have no expiration dates.

273. I Believe:
A sympathy breakthrough is:
- When you care more about someone else's pain than your own.
- When proactive compassion overrides reactive anger.
- When your inclination to hate was overcome by your will to love. – Mark Batterson

274. I Believe:
If we hold out on God, we'll miss out on everything God wants to do in us.

275. I Believe:
The Holy Spirit can't fill you if you're full of yourself.

276. I Believe:
I need The Holy Spirit more today than I did yesterday.

277. I Believe:
Awkward moments can become defining moments if we will let them.

278. I Believe:
If the truth is spoken in love, it can heal your soul.

279. I Believe:
If you want God to do the miraculous in your life, you must unlearn false assumptions. The only assumption you need to make is: GOD IS ABLE.

280. I Believe:
If you want God to do a new thing, you can't keep doing the same old thing.

281. I Believe:
If you want a second chance, seek a second opinion – God's opinion. God's got this.

282. I Believe:
You are never past your prime. If you are still breathing, God's not finished with you yet.

283. I Believe:
We should start acting like an agent of grace, looking for opportunities to love people who least deserve it.

284. I Believe:
Jesus can make your impossible possible.

I love the miracle of Jesus healing the blind man with mud. It's the most encouraging miracle in the Bible. Why? Because it took Jesus two attempts.

"Then Jesus laid hands on him again." (Mark 8:25)

Even Jesus had to pray more than once. What do you need to pray for again, and again, and again?

285. I Believe:

The enemy tries to discourage us by overwhelming us. But I think you can win the battle today. Take it one day at a time!

286. I Believe:

We all have regrets. But what we do with them is up to us.

Don't play the victim. There is no regret God cannot redeem.

287. I Believe:

God's power shows up best in weak people. God chooses the weak to demonstrate the power of His Spirit.

288. I Believe:

Sometimes God shows up. Sometimes God shows off.

289. I Believe:
When we forget the faithfulness of God, we lose faith.

290. I Believe:
When you lose your way or lose your faith, you need to go back to the burning bush experiences in your life.

291. I Believe:
God's answer to our questions is not knowledge but relationship. And that relationship is the answer to every question.

292. I Believe:
If you want a miracle, you must get in proximity of the healing power of Jesus.

293. I Believe:
We should watch and work even to the end of the age.

Leave the times and the seasons with God and go on with your work.

294. I Believe:
Miracles rarely happen on our timeline. But you can trust God's timing. He's never early. He's never late. He's right on time, every time.

295. I Believe:
If you start small and stay consistent, anything is possible for God.

296. I Believe:
God's people should assault the forces of darkness by being salt and light.

297. I Believe:
We shouldn't worry about the results of our ministry. The results are God's responsibility.

Focus on doing the right thing for the right reason.

298. I Believe:
We should be a little crazy when it comes to God's Kingdom.

299. I Believe:
It's time for true believers to start serving in church, rather than just attending church.

300. I Believe:
We can become an unstoppable force for God when we're filled with the Spirit of God.

301. I Believe:
When we are filled with the Spirit of God, we care less about what people think and more about what God thinks.

302. I Believe:
Living for God isn't a sprint. It's a marathon.

303. I Believe:
We live in a day when image rates higher than character and style counts more than real accomplishments. We are impressed with outward appearances. And we are easily distracted from disciplines that lead to excellence.

304. I Believe:
The old axiom, "no pain, no gain," but the path of least resistance is the path of least fruitfulness.

305. I Believe:
"Whenever God determines to do a great work, He first sets his people to pray." – C.H. Spurgeon

306. I Believe:
When God is going to do something wonderful, He begins with a difficulty. When God is going to do something very wonderful, He begins with impossibility.

307. I Believe:
There are two basic types of people in the world:
- Complainers
- Worshippers

Complainers can always find something to complain about. Worshippers can always find something to praise God about.

308. I Believe:
"To live outside of God's will puts us in danger; to live in His will makes us dangerous." -- Mark Batterson

309. I Believe:
The longer we wait, the more we appreciate.

310. I Believe:
When you feel like giving in or giving up, that's when you need to hang in there just a little longer.

"He who has begun a good work in you will carry it on to completion." (Phil 1:6)

311. I Believe:
Sometimes the most spiritual thing you can do is just hang in there.

312. I Believe:
A pastor should be to their church like the father that he is to his children.

The Old Traveler: He who knows the danger of a road is bound to warn others of them.

313. I Believe:
You should turn your worry into worship. And your worship will become warfare.

Win the war over your worries and anxieties.

314. I Believe:
The passage of time alone does not bring healing, but making the right decision can set you on a path where time may then be able to facilitate your healing.

315. I Believe:
"Temper is what gets most of us in trouble and pride is what keeps us there." – Mark Twain

316. I Believe:
There is a vast difference between forgiveness and trust. Forgiveness is given. Trust is earned.

317. I Believe:

Our two largest mission fields are the unchurched and the over-churched.

318. I Believe:

Our dreams for the future give us hope for the present.

319. I Believe:

If you spend your life trying to eliminate risk, uncertainty, and fear, you will miss out on some of the most amazing experiences a person can have with Jesus.

So, how big is your God? Is He bigger than your biggest problem? Is He bigger than your worst failure? Is He bigger than your greatest fear?

320. I Believe:

The purpose of prayer is not to get what you want. The goal of prayer is to discern what God wants.

321. I Believe:

We should never underestimate a single act of compassion. It can change the course of your life.

"What we do in life echoes in eternity." – Maximus

322. I Believe:
The steps of the righteous are ordered by the Lord. Not the leaps, but the steps!

323. I Believe:
Success is knowing God and His desire for me, growing to my maximum potential, and sowing seeds that benefit others.

324. I Believe:
No one can go back and make a new start, but anyone can start from now and make a new end.

325. I Believe:
A little suffering can produce a lot of compassion.

326. I Believe:
Signs don't precede our steps of faith. Signs follow our steps of faith.

327. I Believe:
In God's Kingdom, calling trumps credentials every time. Just be available. "Here Am I. Send Me."

328. I Believe:
You shouldn't let evil defeat you. Defeat evil with good.

329. I Believe:
God's power is the capacity to generate change.

330. I Believe:
God doesn't call the qualified. He qualifies the called. God's calling doesn't require experience or expertise. His calling requires availability and teachability.

331. I Believe:
Partial obedience is not obedience at all in the eyes of God.

332. I Believe:
There is only one thing in the world worse than being talked about, and that is not being talked about.

333. I Believe:
The highest form of worship is obedience.

334. I Believe:
True faith is obedience. True faith operates out of obedience, rather than a sense of right or wrong.

335. I Believe:
God is pleased with submission that leads to true obedience.

336. I Believe:
"Ministry should be bearing witness to truth, wooing the souls that stray, and feeding the faithful of the flock." – C.H. Spurgeon

337. I Believe:
There is freedom in submission and bondage in rebellion.

338. I Believe:
God desires a humble spirit and a repentant heart. He will never reject you if you have these two traits.

339. I Believe:
"He can do...immeasurably more than I can ask or imagine." (Ephesians 3:20)

I don't want to live my life in a way that the best I can do is the best I can do. Frankly, the best I can do is not good enough.

340. I Believe:
It's not our gifting and education that sets the course for our lives, but our choices and our responses to God.

Stay firm in the faith. It's not a mere wonder that chickens flock around the person who gives them real corn and not chaff.

"The Lord keeps you true to truth and you will see His hand with you more and more." – Charles Spurgeon in an 1867 letter to his son

341. I Believe:
We are called to preach God's Word, not to question it or criticize it.

342. I Believe:
Power, next to holiness, is the church's greatest need today. Power without holiness is destructive; holiness without power is dead. We must have both.

343. I Believe:
Sometimes it takes a shipwreck to get us to go where God wants us to go.

344. I Believe:
Sometimes our plans must fail for God's plans to succeed.

345. I Believe:
We must recognize which way the wind is blowing (the Spirit of God) and then respond to it. Don't fight the wind. Don't fight God.

346. I Believe:
Serving God is not a checklist. Serving God is a life list that's never filled.

347. I Believe:
The healthiest and holiest people are people who laugh the most.

348. I Believe:
God seems to be far less concerned about where I'm going than who I'm becoming in the process.

349. I Believe:
We should persist in the face of opposition, control emotional impulses, and regulate our moods.

350. I Believe:
When a situation arises in life that we don't understand, we should follow the advice of Mama Harris, one of the greatest saints I have ever pastored. "Just grace it."

351. I Believe:
Life is too short, and ministry is too hard, to keep score.

352. I Believe:
Your reactions reveal what's really in your heart. If you really love God, you'll react like it.

353. I Believe:
I preach for an audience of One. If I say what God wants me to say, then all the criticism in the world doesn't matter.

354. I Believe:
You shouldn't let criticism harden your heart. You can learn something from it. A hardened heart is the last thing you need.

355. I Believe:
"He sets us free from who we're not, so we can become who we were destined to be." – Mark Batterson

356. I Believe:
God doesn't just hear your words; He hears your heart. He isn't impressed with words, but He is moved by a heartfelt prayer.

357. I Believe:
If you give your heart to God, He'll give His heart to you. Then you can be a person after God's own heart.

358. I Believe:
Changing the face of your spiritual life requires more than a face-lift. It starts with a change of heart.

359. I Believe:
The only way to discover who you are is to discover who God is.

360. I Believe:
Every work of art originates in the imagination of the artist. You originated in the imagination of God. Your God's masterpiece.

"Christ is more of an artist than the artists. He works in the living spirit and the living flesh; He makes men instead of statues." – Vincent Van Gogh

"We are God's masterpiece. He has created us anew in Christ Jesus, so we can do the good things he planned for us long ago." (Ephesians 2:10 NLT)

361. I Believe:
"Science without religion is lame. Religion without science is blind." – Albert Einstein

362. I Believe:
Who you become is not determined by your circumstances. The outcome of your life will be determined by your outlook.

363. I Believe:
You must be transformed. Transformed means to change in condition, nature, character or convert. Changed from a beast to a Prince with God.

364. I Believe:
When you lose heart, go back to the vintage miracles that God has already performed in your life.

365. I Believe:
You owe it to yourself to be yourself.

366. I Believe:
Problems are opportunities in disguise.

In the Chinese language, the word "crisis" is made up of two characters – one means danger and the other means opportunity.

367. I Believe:
The heart is the dwelling place of our true beliefs. Your heart is the real you.

368. I Believe:
A person's character is determined by his motives, and motive is always a matter of the heart.

369. I Believe:
We should see through the eyes of our heart. That's the vision God wants us to have.
"I pray also that the eyes of your heart may be enlightened." (Ephesians 1:18)

370. I Believe:
Your control issues are really trust issues.

The less we trust God, the more we need control.

371. I Believe:
"People are drawn to us because of projected success, but they connect to us because of shared failure." – Rev. Dr. Clay Jackson

372. I Believe:
When you give your heart to Jesus, Jesus gives His heart to you.

373. I Believe:
Nothing is more exhausting spiritually than pretending to have it all under control.

374. I Believe:
Making money is the way you make a living. Giving is the way you make a life.

"Gain all you can, save all you can, give all you can." – John Wesley

"I will keep my promises to you, my God, and bring you gifts." (Psalms 56:10, 12 CEVUK00)

375. I Believe:
God is in the business of strategically positioning us in the right place at the right time.

376. I Believe:
A man without faith is a man without hope. And a man without hope has no dream for the future.

377. I Believe:
Failure is never final if you seek forgiveness.

378. I Believe:
Problems are just opportunities that have not presented themselves.

379. I Believe:
Integrity refuses to take short-cuts. In fact, it almost seems like an endangered virtue. But integrity is the moral glue that holds all other virtues together.

380. I Believe:
God loves to use us even before we feel like we're ready.

381. I Believe:
An opportunity isn't an opportunity if you compromise your integrity.

382. I Believe:
You don't really care about people until you don't care what they think about you. You must be crucified to their opinions before you can really help them.

I want those who know me best to respect me most. That is the essence of integrity.

383. I Believe:
You don't get honor by seeking honor. You get honor by giving honor.

384. I Believe:
"When we think of Calvary, we realize it's the place where: God did His best and man did his worst." – John Maxwell

When Jesus died on Calvary, the devil rejoiced because the Messiah had finally been killed: Oh, but on the third day, He arose. He is alive.

385. I Believe:
We try so hard to impress people, but our attempts to impress are utterly unimpressive. What's impressive is someone who isn't trying to impress at all.

"Every day, I do three things:
- I touch God.
- I touch people in some way.
- I touch something that will outlive me."

-- Charles R. Grisham

386. I Believe:
We can find a place in God where loving Him with all our heart, soul, mind, and strength is all that matters.

387. I Believe:
Jesus simplified spiritual truths. We complicate spiritual truths. Keep it simple.

388. I Believe:
The heart beats and we follow. When the heart stops, we surrender.

389. I Believe:
We should be full of compassion, wonder, curiosity, and energy.

390. I Believe:
If your heart doesn't break for the things that break the heart of God, you need to repent.

391. I Believe:
If you want to be free, all you must do is let go. Let go of sin, let go of anger, let go of doubt.

392. I Believe:
Jesus was a Genius because He had the ability to simplify complex spiritual truths.

393. I Believe:
You will never get to know God by looking at Him from a distance.

You must pray your way into the depths of His power and fast your way into the heights of His glory.

394. I Believe:
Most church problems don't come from the abundance of sin, but rather the lack of vision.

395. I Believe:
Revenge is a dark and lonely road once you start down it. There is no heading back.

396. I Believe:
Without God's grace, everyone is running from something.

397. I Believe:
If you want to make God laugh, tell Him you've got plans.

398. I Believe:
Your reputation is not who you really are. Your reputation is who others think you are. Your character is who you really are.

I worked my whole life to protect my good reputation and to be what everyone (family, church, and organization) wanted me to be. I worked hard to please people, earn other people's respect and love. I worried about what people thought as I labored to protect my reputation. The problem is my reputation is not who I really was.

399. I Believe:
God can inflate a heart with a sense of destiny.

400. I Believe:
God loves it when we fight for Him. But I believe God loves it even more when we let Him fight for us.

"Contend for me, my God and Lord." (Psalm 35:23)

401. I Believe:
God's mercy costs nothing but demands everything.

402. I Believe:
The Lord tests honest people but despises those who are cruel and loves violence. (Psalm 11:5)

403. I Believe:
All of us love miracles; We just don't like being in situations where we need one.

404. I Believe:
We have a microwave mentality about serving God. But we are serving a crock-pot God.

The unspoken attitude of your heart: If God has anything to say, He better hurry up and say it.

405. I Believe:
Intimacy with God cannot be rushed; it must be worked on daily.

406. I Believe:
When God fills us with His Spirit, He gives us indomitable courage impossible to subdue.

407. I Believe:
The best form of love is receiving what God has already done for us, then reflecting that love in our lives.

"Embracing what God does for you is the best thing you can do for him." (Romans 12:1 MSG)

408. I Believe:
Healing comes through tears.

"But the Lord stood at my side...and He gave me strength...And he rescued me from certain death." (2 Timothy 4:17)

409. I Believe:
Loving God with all your heart, soul, mind, and strength is loving God for God. Nothing more. Nothing less. Nothing else.

410. I Believe:
It's not about what you can do for God; it's about what God has done for you. – Mark Batterson

411. I Believe:
If you try to logically figure out the will of God, you'll never take a step of faith.

The will of God is not logical; it's theological.

412. I Believe:
Sin is a waste of energy on things you can't have or can't control like lust, pride, and anger. Then you waste even more energy on things like guilt, shame, and regret.

I heard a Greek Orthodox priest use this scripture in a funeral: "LORD, if you kept a record of our sins, who, O Lord, could ever survive?" (Psalm 130:3)

Thank God for grace and mercy.

413. I Believe:

Fiction appeals to our highest hopes and deepest desires by depicting what we wish were true. But the truth is stranger than fiction.

- Jesus dematerialized and dematerialized. (John 20:19)
- He stopped a tropical storm. (Mark 4:35-41)
- He changed the molecular structure of water and turned it into wine. (John 9:6-11)
- He defied the law of gravity. (Acts 1:9)
- He walked on water. (Matthew 14:22-33)
- He walked through walls. (John 20:19, 26)
- He turned energy into matter and fed 5,000 with five loaves and two fish. (Matt. 12:25)

And that is stranger than fiction.

My mission in life as a pastor is to help people maximize their God-given potential. I see things in people that they cannot see in themselves. I see would-be worshippers. I see would-be prayer warriors. I see would-be altar workers. I see would-be givers of finances.

414. I Believe:

The same spirit that raised Jesus from the dead is at work within us. The Holy Spirit is our sixth sense. He is also our fifth force.

The forces of nature:
- Gravity
- Electromagnetism
- The strong nuclear force
- The weak nuclear force
- The Spirit of God.

415. I Believe:
Everything minus God equals nothing. But plus God plus nothing equals everything.

416. I Believe:
If you take a single step in God's direction, spiritual adrenaline will surge again through your veins.

"God loves with a great love the man whose heart is bursting with a passion for the impossible." – William Booth, Salvation Army founder

417. I Believe:
The Spirit of God should drive your actions, empowering you to live according to God's higher values, not according to the lower values of this world.

418. I Believe:
Faith is trusting God no matter how impossible the odds seem.

Sometimes God invites to us to defy the odds. Sometimes God allows the odds to be stacked against us so we can experience a miracle of divine proportions.

419. I Believe:
You're inclined to believe what others say about you over what God says about you.

420. I Believe:
No matter what you have done or haven't done, God's power is big enough to change you. God's power is bigger than your past.

Most likely you are not yet who you are supposed to be.

421. I Believe:
"The best definition of success is for those who know you the best, love and respect you the most." – John Maxwell

422. I Believe:
It doesn't matter what you do. If it's good and righteous, God wants to help you do it.

423. I Believe:
One can reach the gates of hell just as easily by short steps as by large ones.

"My conscience is taken captive by God's Word." – Martin Luther

424. I Believe:
You shouldn't let what you can't do keep you from doing what you can do.

"Perhaps the Lord will act in our behalf." (1 Samuel 14:6 NIV)

425. I Believe:
Instead of dissecting the scripture, let the scripture dissect us (our thoughts, our dream, our attitude, our desires, our fears, our hopes).

426. I Believe:
God honors spiritual desperados, people who are desperate for God..

I'm afraid the church is filled with spiritual sightseers instead of spiritual desperados.

427. I Believe:
God hasn't given up on you. He can't. It's not in His nature.

428. I Believe:

The way you dig up the root of bitterness is with the shovel of forgiveness.

429. I Believe:

God is always doing a new thing.

Go ahead and build altars to mark the holy moments of the past. But the purpose of an altar is to remind us of God's faithfulness in the past, so we have faith to believe Him for the future.

430. I Believe:

We cling too tightly to what God did last that we often miss what God wants to do next.

God is at work right here right now. Press On.

I love my past, but I won't find a new place with God in the past.

His name was not I Was; His name is I Am. (Exodus 3:14)

431. I Believe:

We should always deflect praise to God. If we don't, look what happened to lucifer.

432. I Believe:
Lucifer's fall shows us that whatever you don't turn into praise turns into pride.
- It was God who gave lucifer his beautiful form.
- It was God who gave lucifer his beautiful voice.

Lucifer started glorifying the gift, rather than the God who gave the gift which caused his fall.

"Lord, don't let my gifts take me farther than my character can sustain me." – Mark Batterson

433. I Believe:
"The deepest form of despair is to choose to be another than oneself." – Author Unknown
At the end of the day, God is going to ask you, "Why weren't you more like Me?" Why weren't you more like you?

434. I Believe:
You must overcome the labels that bind you.

"Don't rely too much on labels, for too often they are fables." – Charles H. Spurgeon

435. I Believe:
Our destiny is to become like Jesus. And to become like Jesus is to become like nobody else.

436. I Believe:
- You're God's masterpiece created perfectly in His image.
- You're an overcomer able to handle all of life's challenges.
- You're an ambassador sent by God to represent Him.
- You are not who others say you are. You are who God says you are.

Live according to God's higher values, not according to the lower values of this world. Don't live a timid, halfhearted, shallow life. Live boldly in the confidence of God.

437. I Believe:
If you give God a chance, He will redeem your disappointments.

Christ gives me the strength to face anything. (Philippians 4:13 CEVUK)

"In this world you will have trouble. But take heart, I have overcome the world." (John 16:33)

438. I Believe:
God is infinitely better than your best thought on your best day.

439. I Believe:
When God sees you, He sees you as a finished product. God doesn't see an empty canvas. God doesn't see a blank page. God doesn't see a marred slab of stone. God sees a masterpiece of art. God sees a best seller. God sees a sculpture of beauty.

440. I Believe:
You are God's magnum opus. His greatest masterpiece.

441. I Believe:
Sincere faith is unlearning the senseless worries and misguided beliefs that keep us captive. Sincere faith rewires your brain, so you think differently.

442. I Believe:
A lot of people feel like they are overlooked and unappreciated after doing so much for God, but God's delayed blessings are His best blessings.

The blessings are coming so keep doing what you do for God.

443. I Believe:
If you leverage your weakness, you will discover new strength.

444. I Believe:
Some people spend their whole lifetime getting ready to do what God wants them to do, then don't do it, because they think they are not ready to do it.

445. I Believe:
When we say God works in mysterious ways, it's a polite way of asking, "Why does God do stuff that doesn't make sense?"

God is mysterious. The more we know, the more we know how much we don't know. The more we know, the greater the mystery.

"Can you fathom the mysteries of God?" (Job 11:7)

446. I Believe:
Sometimes we want to Twitter God and want to reduce Him to 140 characters. But God doesn't fit into 140 characters.

447. I Believe:
We should revel in God's mystery. When we do, worship happens. Then life becomes much more exciting.
I believe there can be certainty in the mystery. It's called faith. The first thing I learned about God is that I just can't quite figure Him out.

448. I Believe:
Growing in my knowledge of God is always an adventure. The more I learn about God, the more I realize how little I really know about Him.

449. I Believe:
God uses adversity to expand our capacity to serve Him.

450. I Believe:
Overestimating ourselves is a problem; underestimating God is an even bigger problem.

"In God's hands alone resides supreme power and infinite wisdom." – The Count of Monte Cristo

451. I Believe:
It's not until we lose what we have that we really appreciate it. It's called retroactive gratitude.

452. I Believe:
Many Christians just go through the motions of life.

Leonardo Di Vinci said, "The average human looks without seeing, listens without hearing, touches without feeling, eats without tasting, and talks without thinking."

In other words, we go through the motions. Our eyes are wide shut.

453. I Believe:
"Unbelief puts your circumstances between you and God. Faith puts God between you and your circumstances." – F.B. Meyer

Faith is not mindless ignorance; it simply refuses to limit God to the logical constraints.

I'm a child of God. I don't want to walk on the path of forgetfulness, nor on the course of ingratitude.

454. I Believe:
Sin has its limits, but God's grace is measureless!

"But where sin increased, grace increased all the more." (Romans 5:20)

455. I Believe:
Worship without knowledge is empty worship. God doesn't just want you to worship Him; He wants you to know why you're worshipping Him.

456. I Believe:
Worship is transcendent wonder for which there is no limit or measure.

457. I Believe:
God isn't as concerned with our level of righteousness as He is our level of gratitude.

458. I Believe:
All worship is not equal. The more you know about God, the more you can worship God.

459. I Believe:
"It is inbred in us that we have to do exceptional things for God; but we have not; we have to be exceptional in the ordinary things." – Oswald Chambers

"The chief proof of a man's real greatness lies in the perception of his smallness." – Sherlock Holmes

460. I Believe:
God defies human imagination.
God is "able to do immeasurably more than all we can ask or imagine." (Ephesians 3:20)

461. I Believe:
Leaders must be led by the spirit of God.

How I love this great adventure. Every day is a new challenge. Every day a new victory. Every day a new opportunity.

"Love is either a great adventure or nothing at all." – Helen Keller

462. I Believe:
"Nothing is more dishonorable than an old man, heavy with years, who has no evidence of having lived long except his age." – Seneca

463. I Believe:
We see what we're looking for.

Look for the good in your church. See the good in your leadership.

464. I Believe:
If you don't have vision, there is nothing to stop the process of aging in your life. Vision is a preservative that keeps you from getting old.
"Now give me this hill country (the Land of Giants) that the Lord promised me." – Caleb (Joshua 14:12)

465. I Believe:
Too many Christians are frustrated by the gap between their theology and reality.

466. I Believe:
We should be the most realistic people on the planet, but I also believe we should be eternal optimists as well. Full of realism. Full of optimism.

467. I Believe:
How we invest our energy reveals our true priorities. Love is not measured by words spoken. Love is measured by calories burned to show how much you love.

"Before you embark on a journey of revenge, dig two graves." – Confucius

468. I Believe:
"If I have seen farther, it's only by standing on the shoulders of giants." – Sir Isaac Newton

I have had the privilege of being mentored by great men of God like F.V. Shoemake, Jimmy Shoemake, George Glass, Sr., Arless Glass, George L Glass, Jr., and O.C. Marler. I will forever be indebted to these great men.

469. I Believe:
God has given you a dream. He has spoken something into your spirit. It's unfulfilled because you're waiting for God to part the waters.

Get your feet wet. Step into your miracle.

470. I Believe:
Once you see God do the impossible, you will believe God to do the impossible again, and again, and again. You must believe it to receive it.

471. I Believe:
Loving God with all your strength means:
- expending energy for Kingdom causes
- blood, sweat, and tears
- sacrifice
- hard work

472. I Believe:
You should quit pretending to be who you're not and start trying to become who God called you to be, a spiritual adventure seeker on the great adventure.

473. I Believe:
The church should be the safest place in town where we can reveal our worst sins. Anything less is hypocrisy.

474. I Believe:
Many people think they must get their act together to come to God. That's ludicrous. That's like getting healthy before you go to the doctor.

475. I Believe:
God delights in re-crafting our sorrows, failures, and missteps into trophies of his epic grace.

Epic grace equals grace that is larger than life and is beyond your imagination.

476. I Believe:
It is the uncertainty of life that makes life worth living. Uncertainty is where faith enters the equation. And that's when life gets fun.

477. I Believe:
"Whoever humbles himself like this child is the greatest in the kingdom of heaven..." (Matthew 18:4)

Part of becoming a child is becoming less self-conscious and more God-conscious.

478. I Believe:
God is so good at what He does that we tend to take Him for granted.
- He is so faithful.
- He is so powerful.
- He is so loving.
- He is so wise.
- He is the ultimate constant.

If you aren't hungry for God, could it be you're full of yourself? And that's why God can't fill you with His spirit?

479. I Believe:
We shouldn't try to prove ourselves to God, but rather ask God to prove Himself to us.

480. I Believe:
The greatest truths ought to be communicated in the most unforgettable ways.

I'm talking donkeys and swimming ax heads.

481. I Believe:
When you have a spirit of pride, people will resist you, but if you have a spirit of humility, you will be received.

The spirit of humility never loses to the spirit of pride.

482. I Believe:
We should guard against double standards. So many publicly preach perfection, but privately expect imperfection. The church needs to accept humanness without condoning sin.

I'm not sure what mistakes you've made or what sinful memories are etched onto your mind, but I know God hasn't given up on you.

www.ingramcontent.com/pod-product-compliance
Lightning Source LLC
Chambersburg PA
CBHW070205100426
42743CB00013B/3053